# epiphany

❋ • ❋ • ❋ • ❋ • ❋ • ❋

## POEMS IN THE KEY OF LOVE

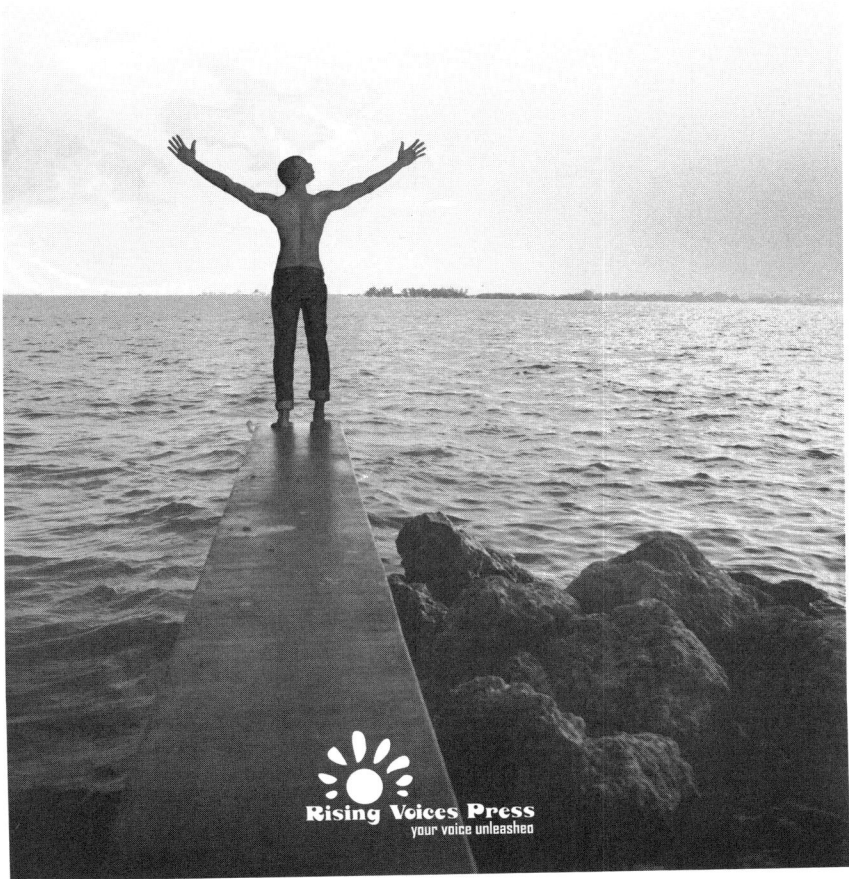

**Rising Voices Press**
your voice unleashed

# epiphany

## POEMS IN THE KEY OF LOVE

# URIAH BELL

**Rising Voices Press**
your voice unleashed

**epiphany**: poems in the key of love

Copyright ©2009 by Uriah Bell

Published by:

Rising Voices Press
P.O. Box 230823
Boston, MA 02123

**ISBN-10: 0-615-34318-X**
**ISBN-13: 978-0-615-34318-1**
Library of Congress Control Number: 2009913610

To Will, he who chose to
love me no matter what, flaws and all.

To love.

# TABLE OF
# CONTENTS

**KEY ONE: YOU AND ME**

## KEY TWO: MAMA, DA KIDS, AND 'NEM

*"(Love) is easily the most empty cliché, the most useless word, and at the same time the most powerful human emotion—because hatred is involved in it too."*

—Toni Morrison

# 1 S T

# K E Y

L ove, this so called many splendid thing, should at times be called this many splintered thing. Maybe I'm preaching to the choir, or perhaps only speaking for myself when I say this love thing is rough. And before you jump to conclusions thinking that I'm on some tangent that every R&B, Country, Blues and sometimes even Hip Hop artist has been on from the launch of their careers, or that I'd be better off writing greeting cards than poetry, understand that by love I mean love on all levels. *They* say that anything worth having at all is worth fighting for, but with love, it seems we fight, and fight and fight, only to find out it is less trial and more error. In fact, many people fight the good fight for the wrong people only to give up on the fighting just as the right one comes along. It's then that our friends and potential right one work so diligently to persuade us to give it one more chance. At this point, we've convinced our own selves that maybe love just isn't for us. Do I have any witnesses? Has anyone out there been through this same cycle, where we believed our first love was our only love? The next one was sure to be the right one; only because we learned so much from our first love, and so on, until our hearts, the strongest muscle in the entire human body just can't take any more pain. We're sure that loneliness or the comfort of our solitude and even our friends will suffice. We convince everyone that we're okay, and over the last. "I'm enjoying this me time, and taking advantage of the dating scene", when the reality of the situation is eating us up inside. Our beds are cold in the summer, and our hearts are jaded and shielded from any potential pains. I know I've been there. I've convinced myself that it was surely only me that could please and not disappoint *me*.

It seems that I've been on this quest of love for quite some time now. I'm not sure if it began when my mother left me as a child; preferring to spend time with strangers, or drugs, or when I noticed that vacant look in my grandmothers eyes when my mother's name was mentioned. Perhaps it began when my father forced my head into the pillow one preschool morning, telling me that there was no school while he and my mother filled the bedroom we all shared with the burning stench of cocaine, or when I began to cry, him threatening me with the belt and fist that my mother knew all too well. All I know is that this search for love has been a battle that has marked me with scars, and flooded me with tears, yet it's a search that I continue on.

I spent the better part of my thirty years so far working diligently to make others happy as a result of looking for love and approval. I can remember never striving for good grades to secure my place among the upper echelon; instead it was to make my grandmother happy. I wanted to prove to her so badly that she had not failed as a parent. I wanted her to know, that my mother chose the life she led, and I wanted so desperately to be her second chance. I always went opposite of what my heart said just to avoid disappointing someone or running the risk of others, oftentimes strangers having to work harder. I craved approval. I was blithely unaware of this behavior until one October night in 2000 when I visited my best friend on my way home from work. It had been some weeks since we'd seen each other and even days since we'd spoken, highly uncommon for us. He, as usual had a house full of others. I spent a few minutes with the crowd downstairs until he excused us both. I followed Dennis upstairs to his bedroom, where he lit incense and turned on some music to drown out the noise from downstairs. For a moment we casually chatted until he asked me how I was doing. I began ranting about my mother, and the drama between her and my stepfather, some minor issues at work, how my grandmother was doing post radiation, my current relationship, school, and so on. He listened intently until I finally had to come up for air. He smiled, held both my hands in his and asked me the most powerful question I've ever been asked. "How are YOU"? This time he emphasized "YOU", and for the first time in my entire life, I had no answer. It seems so simple; a casual, sometimes even rhetorical question that everyone asks or is asked every day, yet this night, in this setting, at this time in my life, because it was asked that way, I had no damn idea how I was doing. This moment in my search for love and acceptance, changed my life. For so long it had never been about me, and because I was unable to answer, Dennis made me promise that going forward, at some point, in every day I would make it about me.

My best friend died nine months later, and I've never known love like I knew it with him. Never before, and not since had someone been truly interested in me, but because of that moment, on that night, sealed with a promise to my best friend, I have learned the balance of pleasing God, then me, and the rest will fall into place. Dennis would say if you can't love yourself, how in hell are you gonna love somebody else? I later learned legendary drag superstar RuPaul coined that phrase, but secretly it still belongs to Dennis.

Love is essential to life. It is one the keys of life. Without it, every day we spend on this earth is mere existing. Love however, must begin with you. Once you learn the power of loving yourself, unselfishly, and unconditionally, then and only then will you understand what it means, and what it takes to love another. Love, as simple as it may seem is the most powerful force in the world. It drove Christ to die for our sins, and when we love someone, we are giving them the power to hurt us. It's a risk yes, but one worth taking, because if you have the foundation of self love, no man or woman, not even your mother or father can break you.

These are the poems in the key of Love….

## LOVE

Do you notice
that feeling when
you lay next to me and
hold me in your arms;
when I loosen up and
press my body into
yours, while we sleep –
naturally?

That feeling, indescribable
unparallel
unfamiliar
unexpected feeling
is love.

When doubts were cast like shadows
from broken hearts of the past,
you let me in.

I was closed off from love, when
you made your entrance, quiet
and unrehearsed.
You had every intention to love me
and I refused your efforts;
found fault in your
blessings just to push you away.

I gave you every reason to
leave, and never return
but you,
instead held me tighter
against my *Will*,
suffocating me with the
unknown, with love.

You called it love
I insisted it was a mess.
A relationship to you
I referred to as a situation.
Far from flaws, but all you need.
You, perfect in my eyes,
but not enough for me.

# IF I COULD WRITE YOU A LETTER

If I could write you a letter
I'd tell you to be careful,
I'm not the greener of the grasses.

I'd make it a 'Dear John' and
sign it 'anonymous', but
you'd know it was for you,
and from me.

I'd tell you all the things
my heart can't reveal when your
eyes lock with mine.

If I could write you a letter,
it'd be everything you didn't
want to hear, but
needed to know.

I'd call my secrets; your concerns
out by name.
Was it you?
Is it me?
I'd leave you to answer that.
But this, I will give you –
I'd close my letter by saying that
of all my secrets, you were my favorite and
my last.

# COMPLICATED

To receive love
without
pending exception
completely.
Genuinely.
Truthfully.

To give love
without
regret
or expecting
or reminding.
Honestly.
Sacrificially.

These are
said
to be
the greatest
of all things.

## HABITUAL LOVE

The burn of a lover's fist,
meeting the eye that once twinkled for him.
Shining, shimmering evidence
that you are his.

Your worth questioned, as
you search for the good in him.
Faint recollections of
being wooed in life's past.

A masquerade,
someone, something you're not.
Happy. In love.
An individual
once upon a time.

The vulgar words you hear
as he pushes himself into
you – mind wise.
He leaves his passion marks
on your body and soul–
marking his territory
like a dog raising his leg
to an oak.

You won't be fertilized.

# WHAT COLOR ARE MY EYES? *(A song)*

You tell me you love me completely, helplessly.
There's no one for you but me.
I believed what you said,
convinced my heart it was true;
outlined a future of love
filled with me and you.

I had my reservations but pushed them aside,
pushed inklings of doubt to the back of my mind.
You asked me the question I wanted so badly to hear,
But those words left your mouth; my answer still unclear.

You're looking for my response, I'm searching deep inside,
answer me this one question,
what color are my eyes?

You assure me the world will be ours,
you'll hang the moon, and rearrange the stars.
You'd work to the bones to make my dreams come true,
you'll give me everything I need, as long as my everything is you.

Hold your breath, spare me the lies,
look at me, what color are my eyes?

What color are my eyes, have you ever really noticed?

You made me love you with false intentions and motives.

What color are my eyes, and what do they say to you?

Can you see the tears you've never noticed, and somehow seem so new?


Do they reveal my pain and disappointment,

in this love that was supposed to last?

Do they give light to the strength inside

that'll make this hurt a thing of the past?


What color are my eyes,

beyond the tears, beyond the hurt?

What color are my eyes?

What color are my eyes?

# HIGH MAINTENANCE

Keep in mind lover boy
that I practice what I preach, and
that I'm well versed and proficient
in everything that I teach.

I may not be a master of relationships,
but I'm no novice in love.
This puzzle between us
shouldn't be this difficult to solve.

You call me high maintenance –
standards, I prefer,
knowing what I want; excepting nothing less,
and yes, sometimes it hurts.
I've given too much in the past
and expected nothing in return,
and if you're serious about this thing we've got
then there are lessons you must learn.

I love you unconditionally, but
I need your love in return.
I can't be last on your list
and communication is a must.
If I ask you to notice me, don't take it in vain,
instead hold me close.
My expectations are not outrageous, and my demands are few,
show me, and tell me that you need me
the way that I need you.

## RECIPE FOR LOVE

I wish there was a recipe for love,
a detailed to do, listing ingredients
and quantities.

Give me guidance on how to
create the perfect relationship.
A pinch of independence
and a dash of hope.

A smidge of letting down your guard –
add trust as needed.
For health's sake, you have
to compromise some pride.

Add a little extra communication
in its place, and you'll never
tell the difference.

Simmer, turning over until
both sides are even.
Remove from heat,
let cool and enjoy.

# BRICK LAYER

This wall,

that once protected my heart,

you're slowly rebuilding

with your lies.

Brick layer,

lay your bricks,

blocking your own self out of my life.

## AMBIGUOUS LOVE

This, the supposed greatest gift
one could receive.
I was told that when you love,
and when you're loved, you know it.
Clear as day,
no questions.

I have questions.

If actions speak louder than words
then he loves me –
he loves me not.
Your words, though intermittent
are silent.
Speak those three magic words.

I love you. *I love you too.*

But we are not kids, and
love is not to be determined
by a vine off of a tree.

He loves me.

I speak and I am
my love for you,
no questions asked.
I love you, but
your love raises questions.
Perhaps you didn't know love
as a child, not able
to recognize true love now.
No more excuses.

He loves me not.

The ambiguity of your
love is not my style,
and the boldness of my
love scares you.

Do you love me?

Do you love me not?

## OVERNIGHT

You say that it's okay to miss you
healthy even, but you
don't understand the void that I
in my poetic prowess am unable to explain.

When you're away from me,
everything that I want, but can never seem to say
comes rushing at me, and when I lean in to tell you,
in my 'ah ha' moment of communication,
the reality of your absence hits violently
and I scurry to find a pen and paper to record my thoughts,
but as I write I get over it all.

And in moments, flashing at a pace that puts the speed of light
in the race with the tortoise I find
myself pre-occupied with other thoughts.
The distance that you insisted was okay,
healthy even, is the distance
that has replaced you.

## SIN

Sins fruit ripening to perfect fruition,
it's nectar sweet and satisfying.
To suck on sins seeds,
becomes euphoric, losing myself
in yourself, uncontrollably.

Helpless moments when your tongues
taste buds become numb, and
your mandible restless.
Still you continue to savor your sins sweet flavor
until you've accepted sin and all of its sweetness
into you, seeds and all.

And then you realize the fullness of its juices and
the realness of your potential.
And though bare, you hold its
sweetness on your tongue until
you've swallowed the last one,
and you,
and sin are satisfied.

## TRUTH

When we're lying in bed
and our legs intertwine
naturally where we're
not cutting off one another's
circulation, it gives me
the impression that you
were made for me.
When I look into your eyes
and the distance there,
I blindly see the truth.

## NEED

I woke up horny so I
took care of my business,
not a ritual for me, but
this Saturday morning
something was different.
You were lying next to me.
I could've reached over
to touch you, or I could've
invited you to touch me, but
then my desire would have
waned.

# FOLLOW YOUR LEAD

You tell me I'm cold and indifferent,
not the me I used to be.
You believe I'm acting strangely,
but I'm only following your lead.

You find no fault in your actions,
instead the blame's all on me.
I don't communicate my feelings,
and I'm following your lead.

Follow my lead
and tell me goodbye,
don't worry about tears
cause none will fall from these eyes.

I'll follow your lead
and dance to my own song;
assume I'll be here forever,
and you'll be wrong.

Go on with your life my love
and don't dare worry about me,
I've been down this road before
of heartbreak and misery.

I'll look forward to my tomorrows
and wish you the best in all you do,
keeping hope for love to come,
praying that next time it's for me.

Taking heed from you and all past loves lost,
re-evaluating what it is I truly need.
Taking the first step to happiness
and following my own lead.

# FULL CIRCLE

Cascading differences
elope to become one.
Tongues untied uniting
in perfect harmony.

The privileged suffer,
silver spoons melt
into plastic sporks.
And now you notice my love.

## FITTING IN

I ask to hold your chain in the mornings
before we part for the day,
to ensure your return.
The golden links that you saved for
mean so much to you,
a symbol of you... is there room for one more link?

Let me be the history in your locks –
the steadiness of the existing, and
your new growth alike.
Individual and distinct, yet
a part of your whole self.

If I could, I'd ask to be the
movement in your dance, for I know
you'd never part with a single step.
The very essence of your happiness
versatile to every rhythm.
make room for a partner,
choreograph with me, and let's give the world a show.

Fit me into your dreams,

make me a part of your passions.

Is there room for my love?

Pay attention to my needs.

Create space for one more joy,

unfathomable,

intangible joy.

Love me, like I've been loving you.

## WHILE YOU WERE OUT

While you were out with your friends,
you asked that I respect your time.
I paced in my loneliness to
get you out of my mind.

While you were out working late,
you couldn't get to your phone,
I was busy making my place
our home.

While you were out in your world,
Ours was diminishing.

# TRUST

Trust has been
an issue for me
from the beginning
of us.

A past of betrayal;
present scorn,
trying not to let
the past dictate the present.

I questioned you repeatedly.
Speculated,
simply afraid.
Until one day, 'trust' surfaced
and your freedom emerged.

My trust in you, as promised
is simply me
no longer caring.

## THE GAMBLE

The trouble with love
on any level is
no matter how you play your hand, or
however close you keep your cards,
you will inevitably get hurt.

In love, the chips will be down
and they'll stack high, and it will seem
best to walk away before
you've lost it all.

## LETTING GO

I'm allowing myself to let go
of what I once thought was good.
Pain's not supposed to come
from love.

And withdrawing from you is
what will shield my heart.
I've given you control,
your promise –
you've broken.

You're holding me back from
what's good for me, and
the pain has spoken.

# WHY DO YOU LOVE ME?

just

answer

the

damned

question

for

once

Will

you?

# MANUAL

If I could, I'd write a manual
on how to love me.
It would outline my
complexities, and
forewarn of all my moods.
I would have it copy written,
and never put into
production, giving you
all rights.

It would be an idiots guide
on loving and healing
a wounded heart,
so afraid to trust.
Because I'm sure it'd be
such a complicated read,
I just might have an audio book version
so you can refer back to.

I would have a quiz
at the end of each section
to gauge your comprehension,
with a bonus question at the end.

*Do you respect me?*

It would explain how when
I'm scared, I never open
up, but rather withdraw into a
place that only I'm allowed.
And how on the inside I'm
so fragile, but refuse
to let it show.
It would illustrate that while
the worlds persona of me is different,
when I come home
I don't want to make any
decisions, and sometimes
to make the day worthwhile
all I need is your embrace.

*Do you trust me?*

It would force you to see
how well I handle you and me;
your clients et al.
And how if you simply called
me once in a while without
want or need, oh how
smoothly our conversations would go.

*How was your day?*

This manual would give
insight on my dry sense of humor,
and how there's always some
seriousness to what I say.
I'd have certain pages
bookmarked, and
key points highlighted.
Take note of anything
in **bold.**

*Who is he, and what is he to you?*

If I could, I'd write a preface
telling you in advance how
much you mean to me, though
sometimes I have a funny way
of showing it.
I'd tell you that I'm willing
to compromise, as
long as you're not made of steel,
willing to yield to me.

*Is this forever?*

I'd tell you that I too
enjoy a compliment once
in a while, and
that all feedback is welcome
as long as it's not all 'constructive'.
I'd define communication
as a pathway to honesty,
trust and longevity as
long as each party
does so in tandem.

*Do I look nice in this outfit?*

If I could, I'd write all this down
for you.
We could start
over, but this, I cannot
do, for it is years too late.
All I can do is hope you
read this poem, and
finally understand what
I've been asking of you
since the day you made
me fall in love with you.

*Do you regret it?*

# THE INVITATION

It started with a simple wink;
couples play.
A test of language, communications –
no barriers,
followed by an exchange of information;
a game we know all too well.

Compliments – harmless, then sexual,
disrespectful, especially because
your other half doesn't know.
You feign fatigue, a simple goodnight
kiss on the forehead,
Then you creep.

Text messages continue,
followed by a phone call.
harmless couples play, less the
couple leads to his arrival.
You're awake when your love
rises from bed, good timing.
You kiss him on his forehead,
saying "I couldn't sleep".

## eLOVE

The  kids chat online,
some say only looking for friends.
No fats, no fems,
my 'friends' have to look a certain way.
Profile pictures include photo shopped,
cropped faces, complimented by
exaggerated enlargements of his anatomy.

There's an exchange of emails, and
if you're sexy, NOT substantial – phone numbers.
Driven by flesh, they meet in dreary house balls, and
bathroom stalls, and
immediately are in love

Empty inside, one never returns
the others calls.
You see, there just wasn't that connection,
so he logs on again in search of
that special someone.

## CLOSE ENCOUNTERS

Five relationships in the past, and
more concubines than I care to, or
am able to recall, and I've
just learned that every man
who has kind words doesn't
have a motive of love.

Wanting so much to be held
that we convince ourselves
every smile is a warm embrace.

The foolish self-trickery of love
allows us to justify juxtaposing
love and lust, and
believing the two somehow
are the same.

Loves two faces of
heaven and hell, and
somehow we head for the darkness.

If I could reach out and
hold the frame of your silhouette
and move slowly to
the music of your silence...
we'd be as one.
My imaginations perfect pairing, and
my dream everlasting love.
If I could push the thickness of
my love into your heart, you'd
learn the words I could never speak.
But alas, your silhouette is a figment
of my desires, moving too fast
to find my love.

## MEN

In my many failed

attempts at love,

I've come to look at

men as the mere

sex objects they are.

Good for nothing but

heartache, and

failed expectations.

And if I'm lucky

twelve minutes of

"yea, you like that baby"?

And just as

they feign potential

to be more, I lie and whisper

*yes.*

## TONGUE-TIED *(A Trilogy)*

He was so fine he made me
swallow my gum,
not like any other man
I've seen here.
I was stunned and confused,
breath stolen away
by his swagger –
masculine and into me.

I must've looked stupid –
unable to verbalize anything.
Just dumbfounded by this
man.
I wonder if he's looking
at me the way
I'm looking at him?

I'd passed him many
times before but
never took notice,
until today.
Him in his white jersey shorts
stretched legs,
and surrendering smile.

I wanted to reach out
and touch him,
see if he was real.
Learn of all his
insecurities and tell
him not to worry
I got you…

I just knew he was
a figment of my imagination
a mere aftertaste lingering
on my palate.
He walked past me,
I could smell him like
smoke rising from
jasmine incense.
Burning eyes and suffocating, but
we light them anyway.

He smiled, giving me
the invitation to speak, but
tongue was tied,
lump in throat –
I simply cannot speak.

He must think me

a fool,

so he exits,

evacuating himself from

me like so many

of them do.

## TONGUE-TIED *(part two)*

He wore black sweats today,
his musk still sweet in my
enflamed nostrils.
Evidence that he was just as excited
to see me was revealing itself
like mushroom caps through freshly hydrated soil.

I played coy, at least in my mind
but my stares told him to speak.
This was to be the day, the
day for all juvenile flirting and
adolescent innuendos to end.

We both wore rings of commitment,
neither of us paying attention to the others
or our own.
Dark features made me want to know more –
craving to hear his voice, like a fiend
for a hit.
How can you crave something you've never
known?

A subtle invitation to step
ahead of him, I could not hear
his voice, his muffled muteness
fell on deaf ears.
I declined,
for him in front
of me was more of a sight.
I'd missed my chance
and all I could think
was *SHIT*.

## TONGUE –TIED *(part three)*

Hot summer day,
him still on my mind;
rollercoaster cascading through
the sky;
screams of thrill and terror.
Cotton candy and fried dough
filled the air, but they were replaced.

Like kismet, he appeared, like
Jesus and the white light, only
he had arms bare, and legs exposed
in khaki shorts lighter than his skin
red shirt, power,
anger,
and sex color.

Me brave approached he,
and like he had programmed
my move welcomed me with smile
and hug – like old friends but more.
His touch sent shock waves
throughout and through in
my body, I gasped, forgetting to breath.

Our embrace lasted forever and
still only a millisecond.

We laughed at the timing
and coincidence of it all.
It was confirmation that
tongue was tied for a reason
and that butterflies still
resemble a crush.

I lay in bed that night
with smile on face,
and rested butterflies.
Uncertain of what's to come, but
relieved that tongue was now untied.

## ENCAPSULATED

The quiet kid on the plane
observing the other passengers,
laughing at the foolishness
and absurdities around him,
crying inside.

He finds both solace
and shame in
the ignorance of others.
A reprieve of his own
insecurities.

Sitting next to the
partner he adores
lonely, they haven't spoken
a word since take off.
Soothing calm consumes
him, the middle man
of the comfort and anxiety
inside him.

He closes his eyes
as he explodes in
laughter,
simply amused by the
fact that they've
sat next to each other;
the trip of their lives
without a word spoken.

## CONFESSIONS OF A NYMPHOMANIAC *(part one)*

Like a hawk with
eyes set on his prey,
I spot you and assess your
anatomy.

Envisioning you – sans
those silly threads of trendsetting
fabrics.
I can smell your
pheromones and
devour your aroma, and
it excites me.

A fabled fantasy, someone
spotted at the mall, on the streets
or at the gym.

My mind races and swells,
consumed with me inside
of you, and what heights we
must reach.

My silly vivid mind, the
mind which allows me to excel
at being a poet, curses
me with believing you'd ever
be more than
a figment of my psyche fantasy.

Forcing me to rush to
my private quarters and release
myself with your aroma on
my tongue, and thoughts
of consuming you.

And my relief though
explosive is not
satisfying.

## THAT GROOVE

You ever experience a groove
so sweet, you just had to
write a poem about it?

I'm talking about that
extreme heat, dehydrate you
kind of love.

You know, that
fall asleep in place,
I'm sweaty but like it so much
I can't shower kind of love?

That – my legs are cramped
I can't go on, but I must
kind of love.

That love so intense, it's a
competition of who's gonna
please who the best kind of love.

That let's be acrobatic, and use
ALL the space in the house
Cirque du Soleil
kind of love.

That can't keep quiet, and
I know the kids are in the next
room
kind of love.

That I'm stuck between
fantasy and reality,
fact and fiction kind of love?

That colorfully abstract,
unspoken dialogue
fat and skinny
thick and thin
smooth and shiny
inhale, exhale
sweet and sour
hip-hop and country
top and bottom
pain and pleasure
make you want to
smoke a joint, and
play with your crayons
kind of love.

All I'm sayin' is......

Damn.

## OUR POEM

complexities simplified through an arguments score,
high notes of double standards
the attention of strangers their divide
like staccato, like stac.ca.to

heavy baggage and painful pasts stop love
love can't flow between the two like yin, like yang
crowded canals of imports, exports; marketplace
but the goods, but the goods can't be exchanged

ever try to coast up 6th ave at a set pace
without catching any traffic lights?
that's what it feels like loving you – impossible
impossible even at 4:01 am on a Sunday morning.
but i try, and try, and try...

what i'm saying is – show me some love before someone else does
let's make our score without staccato; flow with me love
let's trade our goods, quietly, publicly, on the narrow canal of eternity

*i got what you want. you got what i need*

let's tune out the noise and use the traffic lights to
get to know each other just a little more.

## WHEN IT ALL FADES TO LIGHT

What happens when love just isn't enough?

Where do you go when home is no longer
home, and his arms are no longer safe?

How do you justify the absence in a kiss
that was once fulfilling?

How many excuses can you make for the
late nights and missed calls?

When it all fades to light, and
questions are answered, exhale
and embrace yourself.

# 2ND

# KEY

The saying goes "when you come around family, you find love". My family, as unconventional as we are is a direct fit into this statement. I'm on my way 'home' from home in Detroit where I've only spent the last two days with my family (friends included) and as exhausting as it was, it was a blast. I can't remember the last time I've laughed so hard, and cried so hard, and been so welcome. We reminisced on old memories and in a couple short days made some new ones. There was drama, but like the troops we are, we overcame it. Though I moved nine hundred miles away and call the two bedroom apartment that I share with myself home, this trip reminded me that I moved nine hundred miles away, out of the state, to a new place, to embark on new opportunities and every night I simply return to a two bedroom apartment that I share with myself, and that I am so far from home.

For a change, the drama didn't overwhelm me. The rushing didn't consume me. I lost track of all that in the smiles, the laughter, the history. My little sister is a senior in high school and I returned home for her senior pinning ceremony where I'm proud to say, I was given the honor of pinning her. Watching this little girl grow into a young woman has been the best experience of my life. In 2002, as I lay on a hospital bed wanting, wishing, and praying to die, it was her eyes, her passion, her love that made me realize how very selfish I was, and in one drop of a tear from her then, 10 year old eyes I realized I had to do this, and this was so much bigger than me. I prayed endlessly then, and continue to do so now for the Lord to let me see her grow into the woman she's become. As I looked at her on that stage, so poised, and mature I recalled my prayers back then and could only look up, and say 'Thank You'. We all have a story to tell, and so many of us, myself included, go through life without telling it either because we have no one to tell, or just don't know where to begin. Well, there is no better place to begin than the beginning.

As a writer, I am simply telling my story, sometimes even our story, and I encourage people to tell their story too. By telling our stories, we're empowering others to tell theirs. I write because I do have something to say, and I insist that others listen. It's my therapy.

Move ahead seven months, and again I'm on my way back to Boston from Detroit, neither of which truly feel like home at this moment. I guess I'm sort of displaced. Anyway, since the prior entry for my sister's senior pinning, I've also flown to Detroit for Christmas and my birthday – one trip, and now my sister's graduation. I still feel love when I come around family, and sometimes to Detroit but as the dynamics in our personal lives change, it seems that love does as well. Or, it seems, the love that my family shares, for me at least is not enough to go around. I'm certain I'm correct in saying this, as long as my entire family, which keep in mind only really consists of my grandmother, my mother, my sister and me, isn't together at the same time, then the love is there and evident. But throw in person four or five or six, and then the love is selfish. Someone feels left out. Attention isn't being spread fairly, and someone usually leaves the occasion intent on never getting together again. It's absolutely draining. I never understood how families with double digit sibling counts, which turn into aunts and uncles, cousins and great this and that in law, did it. If my dysfunctional mini family can't make it through what should be a special occasion, then how the hell do these mega-church sized families get together for the holidays when you almost have to see one another, let alone empty bank accounts to voluntarily have family reunions?

My family has a history of complications and dysfunction, and if I were to get into here, this would no longer be a book of poetry, but a disturbing memoir, which once read by anyone who has ever heard of DSM IV would undoubtedly land me in involuntary therapy. I am the only male in my immediate family and that alone has its burdens. But, after three decades of spreading myself too thinly, and working diligently on pleasing everyone else, and being in the middle of three completely independent and strong-minded women, I'm just fatigued.

All my life I've wanted my family to get along. If I had one prayer that was for sure to be answered on this day, in the middle of this recession, amongst a blanket of so much despair and sickness and war, my one wish, would be to get my family alone, without cause, or pretense, tragedy or celebration and just enjoy one another's company. There would be no talk of the past, no over analyzing, no favoritism; just the realization that tomorrow is not promised, the past, in this case has been greedily wasted on bicker, and that today may be all we have. My fear is that one of us will receive a phone call of a tragedy and then, after it's too late realize that the dominant memories are filled with disdain, and we'll weep over a casket, or urn, and apologize incessantly – after it's too late.

I don't really have any poems for my family, but this is my message; my wish. And this wish is a poem for family, in the key of *love*.

# FOR THE CHIL'REN

I have to give it up for the ball kids.
The ones who live vicariously through
the crowds excitement.
The ones who work for,
and make, and beg for,
borrow and steal labels
just for the night.
The ones whose juices flow
at the drop of a beat, tada, tuh, ta, ta, ta.

The queens of shade, a defense mechanism
that only the kids know.
The ones that walk for fresh face, and
dipology.
Next to the runway can I see?
Fem queen versus butch queen,
And let's not forget
Realness,
Body, and
HOUSE.

The chil'ren who beat their faces –
create new styles.
Give it their all.
The house mothers and gay fathers,
the ones who find family after
family refuse to accept them.
The kids who go into the world
so cruel and un-accepting, and
insist on being true to self.

This is for the chil'ren.
My sistas, and brothas
walk your categories,
give it to 'em in vogue,
in dance, in shade
in style.

You
betta
work!

# SISTAS

To my sistas so regal and grand;
simply beautiful, with or without a man.
You stand on each other's shoulders
raising one another up.

If I could I'd call you out
by name:
Mary Ann
Winiesha
Maya
Surjourner
Geraldine
our aunts
sisters
mothers
grandmothers.

You gave birth to
the world,
raised civilization and
taught each one of us.
Turned men out of boys
and independent women
from scared little girls.

My sista, Urietta
far from flawless
doing what needed to be done,
to survive; for your
children to survive.

African Queens,
Amazonian dreams.
Sistas from the islands
and main lands
kissed by God's sun
or yearning for more.
Head of the house
or the better half of a man.

Continue to stand on
each others shoulders.
You've sacrificed, days and nights
put dreams on hold,
defined bold.
Looked life in the eye, and
never questioned why.

Coretta.
Amelia.
Neferitti.
Diana.
Those without names,
so many to learn.

## MAMA

You are the core of my soul
so close to me, yet
so detached.

My prayers, filled with
requests for you
have been answered
because you are still here.

I am your legacy
you are my muse.
Keep dreaming, keep being.

My dear mama,
I want so much for you, but
of all wishes granted,
I wish you happiness.

# EMBRACING MYSELF

I let my hair grow after
Obama was elected President.
I wanted to embrace
my ethnicity, (all of it) and was
sure me and my fro would
be protected from the
chains of corporate America.

I woke up on November 5, with
a tear (of joy) in my eye, and my right fist
in the air.
A change has come, and I am
a part of it.

Smooth cocoa skin, a minority by
some standards, but the embodiment
of everything strong
resilient
powerful and
blessed.

Sun-kissed,
full – lipped,
kinky headed
and in control.

I'm embracing my capabilities
and have accepted the pangs
of slavery and
misrepresentation,
a new era is here.

NO is Not and Option
and that is final.
My little sister and
the generations to come
have proof.
Proof beyond the
Civil Rights movement,
and the Underground Railroad.
Don't get me wrong, Ms. Parks
and Sojourner Truth, along with
Frederick Douglass, and Mme. C.J. Walker
Charles Drew, and George Washington Carver
paved this way, our way
but past generations,
and this generation have
been misled by
historians and their books.
This victory is blatantly
in their faces.
Undeniably real,
reluctantly tangible,
and I'm am embracing
the realness of we.

Let freedom ring,
as history is being made.
There is a new décor
in the whitest of houses.

'Ain't I a woman'?
The First Lady to be exact.

Bring out the zoot suits and
let the big bands play as we
celebrate America's
growing up.

I am embracing the
red, white and blue
as well as the browns, and Blacks
yellows and golds.
I am embracing hope,
and change, past
and present, tomorrow
and the next, you
and him, and her and we.

# BABY DADDIES

The cafeteria style
of parenting;
picking and choosing when to be there
and when not to
be around.

Absent during the impressionable
years because those are awkward for
you, but ironically when we need you
most.

Baby daddies.

In it for the moment,
but not to win it.
Straight A's – *my child*.
Captain of the team – *my boy*.
First paycheck – *my child*.

Daddy I'm scared; *daddy WHO?*

We'd call you all selfish bastards
but no doubt we learned all
we'd never be from your cowardice antics.
You made us better men, stronger women
better people because you weren't there.

Thank you, to all the
baby daddies
for hittin' and quittin'
and forcing mama to be daddy too.
I'm happy, successful, on top of the world
no thanks to you.

# NAME CALLING

In the hood, I'm called
bro, nigga,
playa, and pimp.
Son, yo,
main man and B.
In the hood, none of these names apply to me.

At home, I'm bro – bro
baby, son,
Marvin, Uriah
first born, and pride and joy.
All true, yet
not creative or genuine.

In romance, I've been
called love, babes
pooh, sexy man, and boo.
I've been one night, and
long term, today I'm
called single.

In 'the life' I've been
referred to as bitch,
fag, girl, and chile.
I've been butch and fem,

As far as names go, I've
been called them all, and
my head turns to none
of them.

No one has taken
the time to get to know
the real me, for if
they did, I'd be called......

## IN LAWS

Ever been somewhere you
didn't belong?
Engaged in dialogue that was
foreign to you, but you
steadily tried to fit in?
Like an Italian speaking
Gaelic, or a white woman
in the hood.
These are my in laws,
focused on family and tradition.
The womenfolk in the kitchen,
and the men watching the game –
talking about stats and standings,
where I nod and pretend to follow,
hoping this is not what the love
of my life will become.

## "D" DAY

You stopped embracing me with kisses,
hugs then had to suffice,
you gave the toilet seats a double take.

You proclaimed, ' I love you just the same'
promising nothing had changed
but the distance grew greater that day.

I was your everything, your pride and joy,
now I'm your pity party
plagued by stigma.

I understand your disappointment
so understand my fear,
my overwhelming need for your love now, more than ever.

Our bond was solid, indestructible by racism,
addiction and second chances,
but perished that day.

## WAILING WALL *(for those lost to AIDS)*

Let's build a wall, and make it high.

Let's build a wall and let it span the length of the Nile.

Let's build a wall, tall and long, made of indestructible material
like hope; like faith.

We must build this wall by hand, no machine
mass produced facilities.
This wall will be sacred, kept alive by prayers.

We will all kneel by our wall.
We need to cry; remember; give thanks.

We must weep for those stricken in
experimental days, before Sustiva,
Epivir, and Zerit.
Before understanding and compassion,
before AIDS, when it was G.R.I.D.

We must wail for those too scared to seek treatment,
or diagnosis, or
those who simply find out too late.
We must mourn for those without private insurance, or with
doctors unknowing.

Let the band play on.

Jubilant, ear shattering, we will be heard band.

Play on.

We must weep for

Osotto

      Essex

              Arthur Ashe

                    LeBron Moseby

                        Willi Smith

                              Howard Rollins

                                  Ryan White

                                      Eazy E

        Me

              You

                  Mankind

Kneel before this magnificent structure, and

carve your hurt, your pain, anger and worries.

Wail on my brothers, it's okay – your tears are safe here.

Wail on my sisters, your burdens are too great to bear alone.

Wail.

Wail hard.

Wail alone, or

together.

Get it out for those names unknown,

get it out for those who are numbers,

get it out –

Sob

Cry

Bawl

Weep

Wail

until there's a cure, and after.

## MAMA'S BOY

I challenge you my sista,
my Christian sista, to
get to know me and you'll learn
that I am a positive brotha, and
no I don't mean test results positive.

I am educated,
I am worldly,
my sista I am a positive influence
in the lives of all I touch, and like
you, or shall I say
unlike you, I am a Christian, not
because I'm perfect or holier than thou,
but simply because I am forgiven.

My sista, you are escorting your
son out of your life, because
he like Christ – has open eyes and
he is learning to love and love
everyone with heart
wide open.
Do not get wrapped up and
conflicted with who I choose
to love –
jeopardizing
your relationship with your
first born, your
man of the house.

You my sista, who

should embrace your child,

because family, like

only they have the power to do,

turned their backs on you, when

you were not looking and

violated his man – then boyhood, and

now you make me with my

prose and verse,

lyrics and rhyme

guilty of this crime.


I'm culpable of being the role model

he never had, no doubt because

you scared them away with

your guilt.

No, no, no,

I've been trying to keep

his mind clear, and his head straight

so that he can get you

and his brothers, up

out of the inner city gutter,

where bars line your windows,

and you're awakened by gun fire.

It's not me, the queer that
influences him, it's me
the brotha that has seen the
worst, and made the best of
this world I've been given.
A testament, that rising
like phoenix from flame
is no longer a myth or cliché.

You say, you don't want my
literature, my
devil's work in your house,
my book, or your boy, has to find
their way out?

Would I be genuine, if I didn't
speak to all sides of me?
the black side, as well as
the gay side, on top of the
scared side, coupled
with the Christian side.
What's not okay with me
being true to, and loving me, and
discussing the realities of we, while
you, can force your gospel on
the deaf ears that it has created?

You are violating the very amendment

that you and I are exercising.

I am not the predator,

but you are the creator, and

editor –

careful, your ignorance and trepidation will

run him into the very arms

that keep you up at night.

# 360 DEGREES

The irony of this situation
we call life is, no matter
your circumstance, the reverse
will visit you for an
extended stay.

Some call this karma,
but whatever you consider it
be knowing that
you will meet at 180,
then complete
life's circle.

Inevitably, the rich
will scuffle.
Those who serve will be served.
He who gives orders will
experience servitude.
Those who take will lose.

Life, secretly promises us
we will experience all of it, unless
we are senseless enough
to encompass ourselves in
make believe solitude, and
even then such is the circle complete.

## TOTHESISTASITTINGINTHESUN OUTSIDEOFTHEAIRPORTALONE....

Sista,

       I am loving your swag,

               elegant and graceful sista.

                      Confident, sitting, sipping

               your tea, naturally – solo.

     Comfortable in your sun-kissed

                  skin.

               Locks loosened by time,

     Kimetic tattoo on

the inside of your left ankle.

     Elegant, sophisticated sista.

                  Natural.

          Beautiful.

     Comfortable.

Sista.

## MY BROTHER'S KEEPER

I'm supposed to be down for you
and your adolescent ways, but
how can I support your irresponsibility
and the games you play?

Leaving your women to fend
for themselves, questioning
their femininity instead of your manhood.
Being both mama and daddy to the one
you said was your lil' man.

Sitting on the corners smoking herb
and rollin' dice
complaining about this shitty hand
you were dealt, and all you had
to sacrifice.

Taking the easy way out,
giving brothas like me a bad rep,
stereotypes, and casualties of hood wars
stigmatized by statistics.

Laying up in your mamas house,
expecting handouts,
bankin' on dicking some other chic
so you can lounge up on her couch.

Get your ass up, and be a man
instead of succumbing to the
trauma you've inflicted on yourself
waiting on the world to repay
what it is you say they owe you.

# MA' DEAR

I loved you dearly, and
you always returned that love.
You never judged, only praised me.

I remember your cinnamon toast
and though the preparation was
nothing intense, the love
that went into each piece made
it extra sweet, and special.

We had our secret meetings
where you'd tell stories, and
we'd eat junk food,
although you weren't supposed to.
I never outgrew those days
but my actions proved otherwise.

I am so sorry to see you go, but
not nearly as sorry as I am
for letting your son,
get in the way of our
relationship.

As you look down on me now,
just know, and the Lord can
reassure you, that
you did nothing wrong –
not in the thirty years you
graced my life.

# WHERE I'M FROM

I'm from food stamps and eviction notices
stray pets and substance abuse.
I'm from hand-me-downs and second hands stores.

I'm from bi-racial, and multi-races;
Irelands famine, and
Amistad's torture.

I'm from the North and South,
Black bottom and after hour joints.
Chitlin' Circuit dreams, and fears.

I'm from fried smelts and smothered potatoes
mama being mama and daddy.
I'm from thick-skinned women making
a way out of no way – tellin' it how it is and layin' it down.

I'm from cocaine burning, and
daddy giving mama a wired jaw, and
up until I was eight,
I'm from mama going back for more.

I'm from Anita Baker blasting on the speakers, with
Pine-sol shining the floors.
Windows open on a summers day, with me
just once in a blue moon being a kid.

I'm from black blue skies, like mama's eyes

I'm from a purgatory, falling between

the good and evil of reality and make believe.

# 3RD

# KEY

So you've made it to the end of this journey of love, and perhaps the most important section of this book. You've encountered some broken hearts, infidelity, trust issues, family drama, disappointments with not meeting societal expectations, and still you're here. Why, because the most important of all aspects of love, is self love. It's taken me 30 years to truly learn the power contained within me, and to learn that with the exception of God's love and approval, no one else's really matters.

In the following pages, I get a little selfish, some might say arrogant; I get a little real. I talk about some of the taboo things that we tend to shy away from, but need to be addressed. In the following pages I expose myself a bit more; each of the following pieces gives a little more insight into who I am, and at times how I feel.

We human beings spend so much time working toward love, and acceptance, and really have no idea what we're fighting for, or what acceptance really looks like. Love and acceptance cannot be incorporated with ifs, ands, buts or exceptions. I am a self-proclaimed mess. I am stubborn, opinionated, outspoken, sensitive, and at times crazy, but it's who I am, and as soon as *I* came to terms with the sum of my whole, the world had no other choice. If you're on the quest for acceptance or approval from any individual or entity, pull back from your quest, and get to know yourself. Learn your ins and outs, find out what, besides acceptance from others make you tick. Once you piece this puzzle together, wear it proudly. You'll learn that those people in your life that are deserving of being there, will want to know every facet of you, perhaps not all at once, Lord knows I can only be taken in doses, but they will take you for who you are piece by piece.

For too many years I put myself at the end of my own line, and if you ask me anything about those years I can only tell you about self-loathing, and those are years that I'll never get back. I hope that you have found your center prior to reading this book, and if not, I hope that this book helps you to find your center. For me, it was an *Epiphany*.

These are the poems in the ultimate key, the *key of self love*.

## REDISCOVERY

When I was a child,
I was determined to swim across the
entire ocean, and
nothing, not the tides,
nor fatigue, not even
the life beneath would stop me.

When my mama was more into
her pipe than me,
I would stop at nothing to
make her notice me.
And nothing, not her men, or her dope
would get in the way of me loving her.

When I admitted to the
world that I love men,
I vowed no disease
or stereotype would stop me
from being successful.
No love would force
me to lose myself, and
no lifestyle would define me.

When I was confronted head on,
with the shadow of death,
I looked him in the eye,
and declared "I'm not ready"!
He hastily laughed at my
temerity, then left.

What I'm trying to say is,
today I have no regrets.
The other side of the ocean is
still only a lap away.
I still love my mama, and
she loves me today.
The drama of this lifestyle has
not caused me to stray,
and sickness and death have
found another place to play.

## SWIMMIN'

I can't go one day
without your good
lovin'.
It's like finding the
perfect rhythm in
the race.

Not coming up for
air on the stroke
of your freestyle,
and suddenly I'm in
a panic and
drown.

## PRIDE + PREJUDICE *(a dedication)*

Racism + Bigotry

Miscommunication + Expectations

Careless + Sloppy

Greed + Selfishness

Failure + Circumstance

Discrimination + Lies

Bitterness + Judgment

Synthetic + Disposable

Pride + Prejudice

You expected me to lose

every bit of myself to make you

successful.

Living by your standards

was not an Option so

you took retaliatory vengeance

ruining my name, or

at least you tried.

You're just an organization, flawed

but too weak to admit it….

And only because the Judge me told to

here you shall remain nameless.

# FOR THOSE NEWLY DIAGNOSED

That moment you're called into the office
will undoubtedly be the most numb you'll ever sense.
You'll experience feelings of questioning and denial, but
ultimately accept its reality.

The numbness will surpass that first love lost,
when you were sure you couldn't go on.
The news will unquestionably come at a time
when you're on top of the world.

Overloaded by fear and doubt, and all hope is gone.
No matter what your past is, you'll wonder for days; *who*.
And after all the tears have collected you'll accept its truth.

To those newly diagnosed, hold tight to faith.
This is no death sentence, merely a wakeup call,
an obstacle; Gods way of putting you through the fire,
only for you to emerge as pure and priceless as gold.

The most important thing to learn, is that you are not dying,
merely living in a new light.
Suddenly the sky's blue means more,  being awakened by the birds singing
is no longer annoying, but a blessing.
The snickers and whispers of others are grains of salt, washed away by
your rebirth.

Instantly, positive becomes positive and your world is reversed.

When you first hear those words, and you have no idea where to go, who to tell, what to do – this is your second chance.

This is your new opportunity to right the wrongs, get closer to God and yourself.

Listen to the birds songs, and your heart.

This is your chance to forgive, as you've been forgiven.

This is your moment to take control of your life.

When you first hear that diagnosis, use it as your permission slip, and all access pass to live.

# BLACKFACE

Standing alone, or in a crowd
do not confuse this black face
with misfortune, or mis-education.

This black face, whether alone or
amongst the masses is the majority,
the odds over comer.

This black face
belongs to your future
and my past.

Decorated with laugh lines,
finding humor
in your naivety.

Kissed by the sun,
protected by the elements, even
your cruel words and vicious past.

This black face is strength,
passion, pride.
God's face, humble.

It's been hanged, and
beaten, pistol whipped
and hosed.
Fucked by circumstance
buried, resurrected
and carried into tomorrow.

This black face, butter soft
tephlon, was here first, and
will be here when you're gone.

Imitate it,
laugh at it.
snicker and snarl.
Tan yours to be like mine,
you wish you could be this fine!

But his God given SPF
doesn't come in a can.
It's mine naturally, and
what you try to be,
I, we be
effortlessly.

## THE BATTLE WITHIN

There's a war going on
inside this vessel of mine
where a test result tells me
that I shouldn't be capable
of the day-to-day,
my non-stop lifestyle shouldn't be.

The church tells me that
I shouldn't praise the Lord
because I lay with who I lay.
I shouldn't be where I am,
because of where I came from.

The constant, nagging battle within,
caused by external factors depletes me;
working to drag me beneath
the surface of my happiness
until it wins.

# THE SYSTEM

with all my education,
and wisdom, I still
haven't been able to figure
out how when I shop
near the first of the month, with
my hard earned wages
(*after taxes*) in
my sweats,
fighting my way through
the lines and aisles of
others in their
premium denim, yet paying for
their carts full of groceries
with my (*after taxes*).
their lax pace,
probably a
result of the calm reality
that we tax payers are providing
for them and their kids.
my agitated and
frantic state definitely
a result of the same.
three hundred dollar denim
and government, *my apology*-tax payer
assistance.

only in the United States,

so divided, would the white faces

of those assisted,

shun the minority

faces of those assisting,

and it be the norm.


this is the system,

corrupt, tainted, divided

and powerful.


GOD BLESS THE UNITED STATES OF AMERICA

## CRASH AND BURN

The ring of the phone,
followed by the message on the machine.
Speculations of the truth;
the day I lost control.

Careful planning,
a  strategist to many,
capable of anything.
Who bears my burdens?

The silence that followed
the tri-tone, the repetitious
echoing tones of abandonment.
Nothing.

The giant, with shoulders for the world
to stand on,
curled in the corner of life,
the  fetal position of starting
for the first time.

The world didn't stand still,

or even take a pause.

How selfish!

The day I lost control

of myself.

Life, if it can

still be called such

continued on.

## THE LIFE OF A POET

From the outside looking in
it appears that us poets are
so hip, and cunning.
Able to form an opinion
from anything, and
turn it into verse.

Observant and creative,
a gift.
Educated with no boundaries, there
is no subject-verb agreement
in poetry.

I'm often asked my opinion
regarding things that
I couldn't care less about.

The truth is we poets, are so hurt
so bruised, turned introverted that
we write, simply because a pen
is the only thing that understands us, and
paper is the only one we trust.

# A NIGHT OUT

I went out tonight,
went to my closet, dressed
myself in some of the nice clothes
that have decorated the
colorful chamber for
months.

I met good people with positive
personas, and no agendas,
and had drinks, and danced.
I got excited at the life that was
going on without me.

The music was good, and so
were the drinks, and so was the time.
I don't regret that I have to be at work
in four hours.
I needed this, deserved it even.

And the lesson learned is
that life will, and has gone
on without me.
I deserve to live, instead of
merely exist.

## STEREOTYPES

The white boys look
leery when I
approach the court.
A feeling of uneasiness
and tension.
Their best game
is now on.
Will I ask to join
and show them
how it's done?

Humiliation at its best.

Tricky lay-ups
and smooth dribbling!
I laugh to myself,
calm down boys
I say.
But I'll
challenge you
to a game of chess.

## JUST A THOUGHT... *( I couldn't find a title for this one )*

I've always paid attention
to my surroundings, and
followed the rules;
**"Don't feed the animals!"**

Acutely aware of what was
going on, and clear of what was expected
in any common area –
**"Please wipe down equipment and re-rack weights after use!"**

It was common sense to me
to not litter, and show respect,
a simple act of pride –
clean up after myself and
dispose of things properly.
**BIOHAZARD!!**

I'd like to give credit
or say thanks mom for teaching
me the right way, but
the reality is I am more conscious
of the simple things
to prove that I'm not as ignorant
as  some white folks expect me to be,
and are!

## DREAMS

My dreams, so vivid
in the waking hours while I'm sleep,
but
forgettable when the
morning sun hits my eyes.

Vague remembrances' of
locked doors wide shut
preventing me from passing through.
Mixed interpretations of the
many barriers that life
continues to bring.

The ghouls that chase me,
unbeknownst to me, are trying
to warn me, and protect.

I dream of choking on
my words, unlikely of a poet, but
my mere utterances fall on
deaf ears.
Suffocating silence so threatening
to my very being –

We insist dreams should be
fantastic – fantasies of
make believe heroism and love,
when the science of it all
simply can't be explained.

Are dreams foreshadowings
of what's to come, or forced
excursions of the past, and
why is it that a dream
fades away into the darkness
upon hitting the light?

## ASHY ELBOWS

I always had a
deep opposition,
no, contempt
for those with ashy elbows.
It signifies their
naive predisposition
and ability to
sit and daydream
like some cherub styled
bookend starring at
you from all sides
with a smirk on their
faces – laughing
at how hard you work
while they daydream
gathering dust on
their ashy elbows.

## MASSACHUSETTS

I don't know which is worse,
the natural arrogance of
those born and raised here, or
the soon to develop
holier than though
persona of the bourgeois transplants
who are victims of marrying rich
and turning their backs on the
upbringing that made them.

Segregated by class versus
race, all trash of
the trailers shunning one
another.

Massachusetts, my place of
residence, a sure sign that
the grass is not greener
nor the waters bluer – even
in the Bay State.

Warning to all who are bred here,
and the ones transplanted by
circumstance –
hold close to yourself and your
values, get your
business out of the way
and run back to the open-minded
world of racism and reality.

# THE TROUBLE WITH BEING ME

Being a poet allows me
to trouble my life by
creating these perfect
people,
only to be disappointed when
the *cast* fails to meet
my expectations and
refuse to follow
the unsullied script
that I've written.

The trouble with being
me is that, I'm misunderstood,
sometimes even by myself.
Constantly working towards
perfection, in
this, the most imperfect of times.

The trouble with being me is
that you want so badly for
me to be you.
Unapologetic me,
disapproving you,
tangled in a web of
miscommunication and
failed expectations.

The trouble with being me
is not about adjusting to
being alone, but
accepting it.

# THE UNKNOWN

The darkness of the night,
and the creatures that dwell there.
The thoughts that lurk behind
a lovers blank stare.

The ticks behind
every second we wait –
in anticipation of test results
that determine our fate.

The motives behind
a stranger's introduction,
the weakness felt with
a lovers seduction.

What's held by the future
for you and I;
The stories of the past
in the tears that I cry.

The pain behind
what I try to hide,
digesting the lies
that are held inside.

## INSPIRATION COMES....

I watch each and every person,
animal and thing
that crosses my path.

I observe and hone in on
the very conversation you
believe me to be absent from.

I gather my muse from
the simplest of things
that you take for granted.

I'm inspired by the ignorance of
my people, and
the stupid shit white folks say.

The dirty looks I get from
my own people
for being driven, and
the shock on the faces of everyone else
for being able to discuss politics
and the economy.

I'm motivated to write by love,
and most often pain.
I put pen to paper when
I'm absent for words
and void of all emotion.

Sometimes I'm cursed, and
forced to write when the
voices in my head are in
conflict and only a
scattered poem can mediate.

I used to write to get
the attention of my family and
friends, and sometimes my man, but
no one reads this shit anyway.

I once thought I'd make a difference
with my writing, you know, capture
an audience
and open their minds to art,
but I confused them instead.

A strand of hair can inspire a poem
if it's kinky enough to learn you
about the history of slavery –
then and now.

A snowflake, if explored
deeply will show you
that white is cold and dirty,
and when in its natural form
nothing unique; only water.

What I'm sayin' is that
inspiration can come
when you least expect it,
like the irony of appreciating
the uncertainty of tomorrow,
but taking for granted the ones we love
today.

# THE BOURGEOISIE

I won't let my hair grow
into a fro or locks,
I prefer CNN and MSNBC
over Bravo and Fox.

I'm a descendant of my
ancestors jazz,
Coltrane, Sir Duke
Ella and Lady Day;
those that made it possible
for your hip-hop of today.

I'd rather a cocktail social
with diverse neo-soul-cialites
over basement parties
with E, 420, and fights.

I worked too hard for this physique
so my clothes are built to fit,
oversized synthetic fabrications
fattening the pockets of hip hop
stereotypes– yo' son you need to quit.

You see,

I've explored beyond the four walls

of the womb of the hood

I'm a worldly sophisticate,

well traveled and misunderstood.


Yes, my skin is brown

my lips still full.

I can still get down, but

don't let that part of me rule,

or dictate who I am, or

what I'm about.


I'm still your brother,

your man of the house, and

provider.

Accept me for who I am –

I've accepted your

beer bottle on the door step

dreams.

# HIGH SCHOOL

Rumors circulate
anxieties escalate,
tempers rise
self-demise.

Over-achievers
non-believers,
skeptics and anorexics.

Academic probation
schedule rotations,
nerds and jocks
perms and locks.

College admissions
paper revisions,
skipping class
and getting' ass.

Breaking up, and
making up.
Graduation
mediation
class trips
ego  trips
self-identity
new beginnings.

Lies and truth
callous and couth.
Deviance and lies
midnight cries.

Pain and rejection,
overcoming objection.
Eyes on the prize,
judged by size.
Locker room confessions
childish obsessions.

High school was
simply preparation
for life.

# A SINNERS' PRAYER

*Father God, I come to You knees bowed, and*
*body bent,*
*vulnerable and ready to be forgiven.*
*I come to You, a sinner by nature,*
*filled with anger and bitterness.*
*untrusting, and selfish.*

*Dear Lord,*
*I come to You ready.*
*I am ready to come out of this fire*
*that I've set.*
*I'm ready to emerge Your lamb, strong and*
*pure, like gold.*

*Lord, I bow to You,*
*feet washing, and thankful*
*for all You've done for me.*
*For being my protector, when*
*I put myself in compromising and*
*dangerous situations.*

*Father I am grateful that You*
*chose this sinner to cover*
*with Your blood, and kept*
*the dangers out, while*
*I invited them in.*

*Lord, I thank You for allowing*
*me to remain a Christian,*
*reminding me that while*
*the church did, You*
*never expected me to be perfect,*
*but that when I was ready,*
*I'd be forgiven.*

*My Shepherd,*
*I thank You for*
*the green pastures, and cleansing*
*me with the love of family.*

*Lord,*
*I thank You for today, and*
*tomorrow, yesterday and*
*THAT DAY, when I*
*may have wanted to give up,*
*but Your grace allowed me to see*
*that these and all days*
*are days that YOU have made.*

*Lord I thank You for*
*keeping your hands full with*
*my sinners' antics,*
*for smiling down on me*
*even when You were disappointed.*
*Lord I thank You for the birds*
*and trees, and every trial*
*that You put me in, and brought me through.*

*Lord I thank You for listening*
*to my words, and in time*
*reacting as You saw fit.*

*Lord I thank You for all*
*the wonderful people in my life,*
*and the vast majority that*
*are works in progress but*
*test my faith daily.*

*Lord, I too am a work in progress.*
*ever-evolving, backsliding me –*
*still a child of God.*

*Lord, today,*
*I ask that You remold me –*
*start over as You see fit, this time*
*my resistance is gone.*
*This time, I am pliable,*
*shaping into whatever You so desire.*
*Even still, Lord, I admit that I cannot*
*nor do I want to make it out here*
*alone.*

*Lord, please continue to guide my steps;*
*caution me when the roads ahead aren't safe*
*and detour me through a path of*
*righteousness.*

*Lord, You have blessed me*
*in ways I could not have*
*imagined, and at times*
*did not deserve, because*
*You are my maker, and*
*have paved a road for me,*
*and although I've strayed,*
*You've seen me through*
*to my destinations, and*
*even when the roads*
*were uneven, and my*
*feet hurt from travel,*
*I will not complain, for*
*I am a living testimony, and*
*Lord I thank You for keeping*
*me alive.*

*If it's true the stronger ones faith*
*the more obstacles he endures,*
*then blindly I've always*
*believed, and*
*when I didn't know*
*and simply could not see*
*You've always had something*
*better in store for me.*

*Lord, I've come to You*
*many times in the past to ask*
*for miracles for the ones I love.*
*Asking that You get them through, but*
*today it's about me and You.*

*Lord, I am broken, and sometimes*
*even scared.*
*Today I lay my burdens down*
*and ask that You carry them.*
*I've known that You would never*
*put more on me than I can bear.*
*Today, my load is heavier than ever,*
*my questions are many, and solutions few.*
*I want to start over right now Lord,*
*whole and new.*

*It's not about fortune, nor about fame,*
*it's about my past blessings, and those to come*
*that I reverence Your name.*

*Lord, I'm still Your child, yes*
*even me, and I'm coming*
*to You stripped and bare,*
*ready to start from scratch again*
*if You'll listen to this*
*sinners' prayer.*